Heather Henry

A ROAD LESS
TRAVELLED

Thoughts on life from the
pen of a single Christian

ISBN: 978-1-910719-86-2

Published for Heather Henry by
Verité CM Limited,
124 Sea Place, Worthing, West Sussex BN12 4BG

+44 (0) 1903 241975
email: enquiries@veritecm.com
Web: www.veritecm.com

British Library Cataloguing in Publication Data

A catalogue record for this book is available from the British Library

Design and Typesetting by Verité CM Ltd

Printed in England

CONTENTS

Dear Reader

Welcome to a guided tour along a less travelled road – the one on which single people walk. If you have walked this road yourself, I hope you may find company and encouragement as you read. If you are currently on a different road, I hope you will pause now and then to see the view from a slightly different angle. Whoever you are, I hope most of all that you will look not only down at the path but up to the One who has mapped it all out and Who goes with us wherever we travel.

There are various letters sprinkled throughout this book, many of which are addressed to fictitious people. However, each letter reflects what I'd like to say to some real people I've known at various stages of my life. Some to whom I refer have had their names changed, in order to protect their privacy.

I am glad that you are now joining the tour. This, however, is not the beginning of the road for me and I want to acknowledge the help of some earlier companions – namely, friends who have prayed this book into existence, have advised about some parts of it or have proofread it at various stages. I am particularly grateful to Cherrie Irwin, who has created and drawn all the sketched illustrations, which serve as signposts along the way.

Thank you that you have now chosen to travel with me. I appreciate your company and look forward to sharing the rest of the journey with you.

Heather

INTRODUCTION

I think I was 37. Travelling home in my car one day, I was suddenly struck by a thought. Nothing to do with driving but everything to do with my journey. This unbidden thought concerned not the local journey but my life journey.

'Maybe I'll never get married!'

The shock of it was nearly enough to cause me to swerve into oncoming traffic but thankfully I recovered my equilibrium well enough to continue that particular trip in safety. However, the impact of that thought has stayed with me over many years until now, when I am much further along my life's journey.

At 37, the thought of remaining single forever seemed almost unbearable and totally counter-cultural. Over the previous 10 or 15 years, I had witnessed many of my friends getting engaged and married; some were now parents. It seemed that only a few of us were still unaccounted for in the marriage stakes. Even though I had, up till then, seldom consciously considered that singleness might be my permanent state, I had gradually begun to notice that my biological clock was ticking ever faster and that somehow I seemed to be getting left behind others of my age.

Having now lived almost as long again, however, I can look back and see that there was no need for alarm either then or at any other stage of my life, for God had my path marked out regarding marital issues, just as in every other sphere of my life. It was not my friends' lives He called me to live, but the unique one He had ordained for me. Although it has been perhaps a road less travelled, nevertheless it has been a journey I wouldn't have wanted to miss, and for which I am very grateful to God. I look forward to what may yet lie ahead on it.

THE JOURNEY BEGINS

Like everyone else I know (with the possible exception of identical twins) I was born single. The third and last child of the family, I was considered the 'baby' for quite a number of years. This had both positive and negative results. Being so much younger than my two sisters – or so I was made to think – there were things I was considered not yet old enough to do and I sometimes had to sit and watch as they took part in certain activities. On the other hand, once we had all become teenagers, I was often teased by them because I had been allowed to have something or go somewhere 'much sooner' than either of them had been – and so the friendly rivalry continued.

When it came to boyfriends, the natural order took over and my eldest sister was the first to 'go out with' someone of the opposite sex. I found it fascinating as I observed the ups and downs of her various early relationships. Then my other sister began dating too and life got even more interesting. But never more so than when I realised that this exciting aspect of life was coming my way too and I enjoyed several teenage romances of varying lengths and intensity. At one stage, we wondered if our parents would end up with three sons-in-law with the same Christian name, as each of us had a boyfriend called William! Only one stayed the course, however, and he is now my long-established brother-in-law. I am blessed to have two brothers-in-law and several nieces and nephews, who in turn now have their own children. God has provided me with a loving family, for which I am very grateful.

During school days, there were many happy outings with mixed groups, where we girls often talked about who 'fancied' who and sometimes set each other up to 'accidentally on purpose' end up with a particular partner by the time the evening was over. Being of a shy nature, I enjoyed some of these activities much more than others but often was more embarrassed than excited by some of what went on. I remember one afternoon in school when a certain boy approached me as I was clearing my desk at the end of the school day. Realising he was probably going to ask me out, I fled to the door and escaped up the corridor! I sometimes look back to my fifteen-year-old self and cringe at my behaviour, wondering how different life might have been had I lingered longer in that classroom! However, in those days, I had no serious thoughts about my future or whether I would end up with a marriage partner.

What I was considering at that time, though, was the difference I could see in some older people's lives. I began to observe some whom I knew. Although I didn't realise it just then, several would have considerable influence on me and help to inform my own behaviour in later life. One of these was my Great Aunt Sadie who was an unmarried sister of my Granny.

Hers was a positive life well lived and now I wish I could have told her how much she influenced me. As I didn't, this letter must suffice:

Dear Aunt Sadie,

In some ways I wish I could have written this letter sooner. As it is, I know you will never read it, but I still feel I must write to express my gratitude for your life, which meant more to me than you probably ever realised. Actually it is only in recent years that I have come to appreciate so fully the legacy you left me. Had I in fact written to you before, it would not have conveyed all that I now want to say. Isn't it strange how we view things and people differently as the years pass?

Anyhow, my main reason for writing is to thank you for modelling for me and for others a positive single life. Although you lived longer than most of your peers, I know you never married. I have no idea whether in fact you ever had the opportunity to marry. When I was a child we did not talk of such things. Whatever the case, I just always thought of you as my Great Aunt, the one who lived with Granny. Later you became our beloved Aunt Sadie living on your own, wearing old fashioned clothes but, as we siblings all knew, loving us dearly.

We have such beautiful memories of occasional Saturdays or Sundays spent with you. We knew that church was an important part of your life, so we would never have visited on Sunday mornings. But in the afternoons you were ready for a chat with the adults and a time to involve us girls in some activity. Sometimes it was puzzle sheets, which you had kept especially for the wet days, and other times it was a walk to see the ducks in the park. You always seemed so interested in everything, even these simple activities. I guess that's what has left the impression on me more than any gift you ever gave me or card you sent.

There is, however, one card I do remember. It was for my 21st birthday. The card itself, as I recall, was ordinary enough but inside you had written a very meaningful message to me and included a Bible verse. It was a verse I had never heard before – Proverbs 10 v 22 "The blessing of the Lord makes rich and He adds no sorrow (or trouble) to it." I'd love you to know how important it has been to me since. I cannot count the occasions on which it has come to my mind, nor the number of times I in turn have included it with greetings to someone else. It continually reminds me where true riches are to be found.

Thank you for being faithful in sharing God's Word – not in huge indigestible chunks, but in many little meaningful ways. In fact, that is really how you shared your life. In little ways, but always thoughtful and appropriate. My Dad used to tell us about the calendars you sent to the prisoners every January and the correspondence you carried on with some of them throughout the year. I don't expect many people knew much about this, for you didn't talk a lot about it, but I'm sure there are prisoners' families still who haven't forgotten your input into those lives for good.

Another thing I couldn't understand as a child but still vividly remember was that all our used postage stamps had to be kept 'to give to Aunt Sadie' next time we would see you. I can only assume that that was another of the little ways in which you helped others, as you spent long hours preparing stamps to send to some charity or mission organisation.

Some years ago I became a Great Aunt myself. What a milestone that was. I found it hard to believe that I now had the same title as you, my little grey haired maiden aunt, because I still felt so young! Surely I wasn't that old! On reflection, it is probably true that in fact you were this young when I first knew you, but through my childhood eyes you were always ancient. No doubt to my great nieces and nephews I am also very old. But I trust I may be more to them than just 'the old aunt'. How I'd love to be remembered by them with such affection as you have been *remembered in our family. Not as the one without a husband, not as the odd-one-out of the family circle, but as someone who took a genuine interest in people, whether adults or children, whether relatives or strangers, whether at home or abroad.*

One of my last recollections of you was during your final years of life when you had transferred to the Residential Home. Every morning you could be seen walking down the road to buy the daily paper for the residents who couldn't manage on their own. You were like a voluntary member of staff, they said, because you helped so much! Strangely, I have no memory of your last days or of your death. But perhaps that is typical, as you lived life to the full and it is that which I remember.

And that's why I wanted to write this note of appreciation. Thank you for living a life which was memorable. Thank you for being faithful. Thank you for loving not only me but all those around me. In short, thank you for showing me what wonderful possibilities there are to be fulfilled as a single person.

I trust I may honour your memory in the way that I spend the rest of my time here. And then? Well, then I look forward so much to seeing you again and sharing our stories. I guess we'll need lots of eternity to talk to each other.

With much love,

Heather

THE ROAD WIDENS

Leaving school days behind, I entered Teacher Training College and met a whole new set of friends. Living away from home for the first time was an opportunity to see life from a different perspective. From the outset, I experienced God going before me to provide what I needed. On the very first day, out of all the hundreds of new students at enrolment, I 'just happened' to sit beside another Christian girl, with whom I immediately struck up an easy friendship. We ended up sharing accommodation for the first year and very much enjoyed each other's company.

In College, many couples paired off but I did not meet anyone significant. During those years, however, I was also involved nearer home in various youth activities and camps, firstly as a camper and later as a leader. I loved the mixed company there and had one or two close friendships with fellow campers before eventually meeting a guy with whom I had quite a long relationship. In the end, my boyfriend and I mutually agreed that lifelong commitment to each other was probably not in God's will for either of us and we parted company quite amicably, but not without a real sense of loss – certainly on my part and, I think, on his.

My three years of study passed quickly and I found myself in my first job. However, the allure of the classroom faded all too soon and by the end of my second year I began to doubt my calling to teaching.

Only that my principal encouraged me to stay another year, I would have happily given in my notice there and then. The third year proved no better and this time I did resign. I had no idea what I might do next.

I prayed for God to guide. He did – but in an unexpected way. Again, it had 'just so happened' that in that unsettling third year I had been teaching the son of another school principal. Just before term finished, when I was due to go out into the great unknown, the boy's father phoned me to ask where I was going to teach in the autumn. I told him emphatically that I wasn't! However, after much discussion, he finally persuaded me to go to his school for a period of three months, to cover a maternity leave. Those three months turned into many years! As I settled in my new employment almost immediately, I thanked God for His leading and for the opportunity to pursue the career which I'd originally chosen.

As in some other aspects of my life, in choosing to be a teacher I was once again following in the footsteps of one of my sisters. As time moved on, however, I began to realise that the pattern of 'They do it first, I do it next' was not going to continue when it came to marriage. My sisters' marriages had been ten years apart, so I always felt that I had ten years after my second sister's wedding to find a marriage partner of my own. Some friends did not think in the same way, however. They, and several of my more elderly relatives, soon began to ask the inevitable questions:

"Any word of when you'll be following the family trend, then?"

"You'll be next – anyone in mind yet?"

Each one who asked such questions apparently thought that they were the first to suggest such a thing and were no doubt well-meaning. To me, however, it became both repetitive and a little unsettling. Many of these friends were fellow Christians. As believers in a sovereign God, we trust that He wills only what is best for us and that, in the end, all that happens to us is designed for our spiritual good. So to hear such people strongly suggesting that I was nearly bound to get married (it was just a question of when), and that my life would not be complete until then, was a difficult experience for me at times, not only emotionally but on a spiritual level too. I longed for someone to really get alongside me and chat about what God might be doing in my life and pray with me regarding my future.

As I reminisce about the days of my own youth and young adulthood and the problems associated with that stage of life, my mind turns to the youth camps in which other friends and I volunteered for several years. One evening I sat down to write a letter to one of those friends. I began by reminding her of a particular incident which had happened at one camp…

Dear Cindy,

How are you? I hope all is well with you and the family. I expect Lucy will be back at college by now and the house a bit quieter again! Now that the fuss of Christmas is over I also have more time to do other things and I have begun to mull over a few ideas and memories.

I have just been reminiscing this evening about our time at Llandudno camp all those years ago. Remember the little railway on Snowdon, and the bus trying to manoeuvre around the country lanes? What a lot of memories of the girls come flooding back as one thinks of them, too. What has prompted this letter is the most vivid recollection of that whole week – I'm sure you know what I'm going to say. Yes, the evening we had the conversation with Amy.

I'll always remember how you sat patiently beside that poor distraught 14-year-old, her face wracked with emotion, as she found such difficulty in expressing herself. Up to then, Amy had seemed happy enough, hadn't she? A little unusual, perhaps, but certainly content to be at camp with all the other girls. But then that evening she had burst into tears after the evening meeting. I remember you sitting waiting as the tears flowed and then gently saying to her:

"Can you tell me what's wrong, Amy?"

"It's about what you said in your talk tonight" she stammered.

"Yes…?"

"You said we should obey whatever God tells us to do."

"I did, Amy, that's what God wants from us – obedience to His will."

"But what if… what if…"

At this stage she broke down again and it seemed that she would never be able to articulate her concern. Remember how we waited for what seemed like an age before she finally gained courage and blurted out:

"But what if God asks me to get married?!"

I really think, Cindy, that I have seldom been so surprised and amused at the same time. I still don't know how we managed not to laugh.

The reason I'm writing, Cindy, is to tell you that I met Amy again, quite unexpectedly, over Christmas! She has grown into such an attractive young lady. She was telling me about her job at the airport and all the famous people she has seen there. Her Mum still lives in Dublin, but Amy has her own little flat near Drogheda. It was good to meet her in church and know she is going on with the Lord. She was asking about you – and all the other leaders. I really enjoyed our chat but I didn't mention the night in question and neither did she. I couldn't help but wonder, though, if she had had any transactions with God over the subject of marriage. Anyway, she seems content.

There are probably not many who have had an experience such as we had that night at camp. I guess older Christians are not often called upon to counsel about singleness. These days the much more common scenario would be where a girl reaches 14 and wants to know where she can find a boyfriend, and wonders whether it really matters if he is a believer, as long as he's a good genuine guy.

I know how the Youth Leaders in our day would have handled such a situation. They probably would have arranged a session – or series of sessions – for all the young people to talk about the whole area of relationships, and to discover together what the Bible had to teach on the subject. I can remember evenings of this sort, which included topics such as

- *How to meet Christians of the opposite sex*
- *How to behave as a 'dating' couple*
- *When to think towards marriage*
- *What to do if a relationship breaks up*

I'm sure you had similar teaching in your church? That was all good stuff, all important subjects to talk about, but when you think of Amy, I wonder where she or indeed some of today's young people would fit in? As I've thought of her again this evening, I've got to thinking about how we address the whole subject of relationships with teenagers now.

It is no doubt that in her generation, as in the present one, Amy would be in the minority. Most young people still seem to want to get married or at least to find a long-term partner. But the reality is that some of them will not marry, and a few may never even have a meaningful relationship with a member of the opposite sex. Some may not seek a relationship with the opposite sex at all, but will struggle with all sorts of issues around the idea of same sex relationships.

In today's society it is also, unfortunately, all too likely that of those who do marry, in some years' time a number will find themselves single again. Oh, what a confusing world our young people are growing up in. If we were at a Christian camp with teenage girls these days, Cindy, what would we teach them?

I guess it would be good to address many of the issues I mentioned earlier, but with more emphasis now on the different choices of lifestyle 'on offer' in the 21st century. It would be harder to have to include the Biblical perspective on same-sex partnerships or divorce. But isn't it so important that they are guided back to God's standards for relationships and marriage?

... There was more to that letter but we'll come to that later.

Having completed my training and overcome the hiccup of doubting whether I was even following the best career, I then began to settle into life as a teacher. What a privilege it is to be entrusted with numerous little children and be expected to shape each of their educational lives for at least a year. It is impossible to measure 'success' in such a calling but, suffice to say, I find it very satisfying when, from time to time, I meet former pupils and discover they are now well adjusted adults who remember with affection their days in Primary School. There are, of course, also times when we meet others who were not star pupils. One such incident happened me one evening when I almost literally bumped into a past pupil. I was heading for the changing room at a Tennis Club. Around the corner came a young man in a great rush. We only just avoided each other. As he paused to apologise, we instantly recognised each other.

'Miss Henry!' he exclaimed.

'Andrew!!' I retorted and then quickly added "After all these years, are you still out to upset me….?!"

A most amicable conversation ensued, during which he asked me

'Are you actually still Miss Henry?'

And I had to admit that yes, I was still single. Yet another example of having to explain oneself for being on the less-travelled road.

There are definitely times like that when being single seems very negative. However, there are also many positive aspects to the single life and one of them is the time one has available to devote to activities denied to those with family responsibilities. Over the years I have found this to be both a blessing and a challenge. During my years as a teacher, I was able to help with a Scripture Union Group on a weekly basis. It was such an encouragement to see God provide all that was needed each year to enable it to run. Many children attended over the years and lots of happy memories were made at special SU outings or weekends away. Little did I realise then that in these times God was building foundations for future ministry for me.

At this stage I was also committed to leadership in a girls' organisation specialising in Bible Teaching. I loved that involvement and because I was free of other ties, I was able to devote time to it, not only at weekends but often during school holidays. Once again, God proved Himself faithful. I'm sure I learnt as much as any of the girls may have done, through all of those experiences and I believe singleness uniquely equipped me for that ministry.

It was on that topic that I continued my letter to Cindy about how we should deal with today's teenagers …

Cindy, I suppose it's because I've remained single myself that I'd have to ask if we shouldn't specifically deal with the subject of singleness too. I'm not quite sure how we would go about it, but that's what the mulling of ideas has been about this evening. I'd be interested to hear your reaction as a married person to what I'm suggesting. Better still, I'd like to hear what Lucy's thoughts on this issue would be!

First, we'd surely have to honestly recognise with the young people – and maybe especially the girls – that not everyone becomes part of a couple. I think teenagers need to be reassured that in God's eyes, even if not in the eyes of their non-churched peers, it is okay to remain single. It seems many feel they are accepted only when they can demonstrate their 'normality' by having secured a boyfriend/girlfriend. I'm concerned that unless they have already received the right teaching and assurance, some of today's youngsters will hit twenty-something and feel at best embarrassed by the fact that they do not have a partner, and at worst totally frustrated – with God, as well as with life itself. Then there's the whole question of whether singleness, as a teenager or in later life, necessarily equals celibacy. So many young people today seem mixed up about this. Don't you think we need to do a bit of Bible study with our Christian teens on whether it's necessary to be celibate if one is not married?

I'm sure you agree that positive role models are very important for young people. I feel this is especially true about Christian singleness and I'd love to see more interaction between the generations on this. Look around any congregation on a Sunday morning – I'm sure yours is no different from ours – and you will find a considerable number of unattached adults. Whether never-married, divorced or widowed, many regular churchgoers live alone. It seems to me that from amongst them, there would always be those who would be willing to share some of their life experience with the young people.

If I was a Youth leader either in church or at camp, I'd like to invite a single person to talk about his/her life and, if possible, to become a regular leader. In relating to the young people, he/she could model a positive single lifestyle. Or maybe I'd invite a group of singles and marrieds to form a panel one evening, willing to answer questions on the subject of relationships. I guess this exercise could be of benefit to young people who will become the single adults of the future, but, not only that – it might also serve to educate and inspire those who will one day marry, giving them more sensitivity in later life towards their single friends.

Remember how often at camp we would use Matthew 7 v 7 – 'Seek first the kingdom of God and ...' ? Surely we must present Christ to young people today not only as the One who can give them salvation but also as the Lord who has the right to decide what is best for each of their lives. Don't you think some might need reassured that, no matter what their relationship status happens to be, He can supply all they need and that He wants to draw alongside them in intimacy?

So there we are, Cindy, my random musings on a big subject. Who would have thought that Amy's little outburst so many years ago would have sparked off such ideas in my mind today? Do let me know what you think about the subject of young people's relationships today and if you have a chance to talk to Lucy about how she, as a single girl in the early twenties, feels about some of these issues, I'd be delighted to hear what she has to say.

In the meantime, God bless. It's been great to chat things over with you – and no phone bill to pay!

Love to all the family

Heather

CHALLENGES ALONG THE WAY

During my late teenage years, a young fun-loving minister came to our church and set up a Youth Fellowship for teenagers and young adults. It was partly because of his ministry that I committed my life to Jesus Christ. He was a deeply sincere guy who spoke to us both individually and collectively on many topics. One of these was relationships. I well remember him warning against casual friendships between the sexes and telling us not to waste each other's time if we never intended to marry! He being engaged when he came to us, and subsequently married, we questioned him on many issues and he and his new wife were only too glad to share some of their experiences with us. They gave us wise counsel in a relaxed way and I look back on their leadership with gratitude.

Sadly, not all leaders at that stage of life are so discerning. More recently, a younger man was leading worship in our church one Sunday morning. As he spoke to the children, one phrase he used made me react. After the service, I tried gently to point out to him what he had said. He graciously accepted my comments. Later, because I felt strongly about the incident, I wrote an open letter to ministry students, in the hope of preventing any of them from making similar mistakes. The letter was never sent but writing it helped me to get some things off my chest!

Dear Student

You don't know me. We haven't been introduced. Suffice to say I am a regular churchgoer and I, or someone like me, could be in your congregation any Sunday. I am a single adult, living alone, who loves church and benefits greatly from Christian fellowship.

I wanted to tell you about something said quite inadvertently by a leader in my own church recently and about my reaction to it.

I was sitting happily in my usual seat. The familiarity of the setting and of the service made me content. Friends all around, the usual leaders at the front, the band leading the worship – it was all so cosy, and it felt good to be there.

But how suddenly cosy worlds can fall apart and shock waves can attack. For me it happened during the children's talk. The worship leader (another familiar face) had spoken to the little gathered group of 4-10's, had introduced a memory verse and was now inviting the children to sing. Then he said it – the shock wave sentence.

"And will we get the Mums and Dads to sing too?"

How easily it tripped off his tongue. What an innocent remark it seemed. But to me it was the sudden end to a contented morning in church. For in as short a time as it had taken the worship leader to say it, so the sentence which he had said gave rise to a tumult of negative emotions in my head.

"Mums and Dads" I thought, "Huh! Not again!" for it was not the first time that that particular phrase had made me realise with a jolt that I was neither. I was not, had not been, and by the laws of nature was never likely to be either a Mum or a Dad. I was single…. in fact I was a spinster…. a middle-aged spinster… a middle-aged spinster with no children near me. I was a nobody. Indeed I was an outcast. Nobody loved me.

Thus raced my unbidden thoughts as the leader at the front continued happily to engage the children, and any adults who were willing, in singing a lively chorus. It was some time much further into the service that my mind regained its composure and I once again rejoiced to be in God's house with all my fellow-Christians.

As I drove home, I reflected on several things:

- *the insensitivity of those who use exclusive language without ever realising what they have done;*

- *the power of the enemy to attack when we least expect it – and at a point where we don't even think we're vulnerable;*

- *the significant number of unattached adults who attend church regularly.*

- *But also – the wonderful grace of God in creating the church to be a place where we all fit in and where no-one needs to wear a label.*

I hope my recounting of this incident might encourage you to appreciate afresh the power of words and how they can affect people either positively or negatively. As one called by God to a ministry dependent on the use of words, I pray you will know His help in choosing carefully what you say, both in private and in public.

I wish you well as you soon set out to pastor a church. May the Lord bless you and may your congregation – of all ages and backgrounds – have cause to thank Him for your wise leadership.

Yours in fellowship

Heather Henry

Christian or not, married or single, life is not for wimps. Inevitably, we all must take the rough with the smooth and for some the path can be very rough. Looking back over several decades now, I am thankful that God has dealt graciously with me and I have not experienced too much trauma. Rather, I have been blessed with generally good health, with satisfying work situations and with a huge variety of enjoyable experiences. However, that is not to say that every day, every month, or every year has been without its problems or challenges. Far from it.

Some years ago, on the eve of going on holiday, I developed a worrying eye condition. Diagnosed at my holiday destination as having a macular hole, I found it hard to relax until I got back to my optician at home. At that stage I had little idea what my condition was, never mind how it needed to be treated. It soon became evident that it would require surgery. Some months later, I duly turned up for the pre-op appointment with the surgeon, just four days ahead of the date of my operation. Imagine my shock and delight when he – equally shocked – was able to inform me that I could cancel my surgery because my eye was already healed! Of all the thousands of people who suffer macular holes, I was one of the minute number who experience 'self-healing' during the waiting period between diagnosis and surgery. Needless to say, I almost skipped out of that appointment room and the cup of coffee with which my friend and I celebrated on the way home tasted better than any before.

God is an amazing God. Sometimes He gives us delightful surprises. But we cannot assume that He will always do so or that we can put His ways of working into any box. He Himself has said 'My thoughts are not your thoughts and my ways are higher than your ways.' I was to prove that just a few years after my macular hole experience.

Having already had a macular hole, albeit one which was now healed up, I knew the signs when I began to experience similar symptoms in my other eye! I went to the optician but hardly needed him to tell me the problem. Back on the waiting list I went and watched to see if God would heal this eye too. But He didn't. At least not naturally. This time I had to undergo the surgery and the follow up procedures before I could say it was better. God is good but God is God and He does what He wills.

So did I learn anything from my second experience? Absolutely! I learnt what it was to have God provide for me in every way during my convalescence. From a kind friend who opened her home to me for the days when I could not manage on my own, to other friends and relatives who cooked for me or did shopping, to some who offered me lifts when I was unable to drive, to many who sent cards or made phone calls, I was overwhelmed with His goodness expressed in so many ways. He did not take the challenge away but He certainly saw me through it.

On more mundane days, when I am perfectly well, there have been many times when I have longed for company when none was immediately available. This became a more acute problem following the passing of my dear Mum with whom I had lived for many years. In the immediate aftermath of her death, not only did the house seem very empty but, at times, so did my life. A friend once remarked – and it is so true – that as a single adult you can always find someone to do something with (go to a show, have a walk, play a game of golf) but the difference is we don't have anyone just to do nothing with. Life can be lonely. In thinking of these things one day, I found it therapeutic to write a letter to my late mother to tell her how much I miss her.

Dear Mum,

How I wish I could just tell you these things straight to your face or even hand you this letter. But of course I can't, so I'm helping myself by remembering some of the times when that was possible and life was vey different.

You probably wouldn't recognise some aspects of the world I now live in. So much in society has changed during the years that I've been here on my own. Would you ever have thought that even the soaps on TV that you used to enjoy would now include characters who are transgender? You wouldn't even know what that means! And seeing shops busier than ever on Sundays is another way you would be shocked. Oh, and just this year, Northern Ireland passed a law allowing a more permissive attitude to abortion than any other country in Europe... and we're not in the European Union any more... and the politicians at Stormont didn't meet at all for about 3 years... and... I don't know where to stop! This certainly is a different world.

Of course, life for me personally has also changed. For one thing, I really miss you for chatting about these sorts of issues together. You had such wisdom and you never seemed to get het up about too much. Yet you let me rant on when something bothered me. Now, without your calming influence, I know I sometimes worry unnecessarily or 'take it out' on someone else just because I have no-one to listen to me in the safety of my own home. On days like that I hate the empty house.

You would be glad to know, though, that there are some positive aspects of my changed lifestyle. Believe it or not, I've even learnt to cook a bit! At times, I try to entertain others but not often as it's quite difficult to be both host and cook all by oneself. And, as you realised after Dad died, it's not so natural to invite couples when you are on your own. So I usually restrict guests to small numbers. For family gatherings I usually leave it to others. You were such a good homemaker – it's lovely to remember all the happy times we enjoyed together as your family. You always seemed to be able to produce delicious meals and I know I'll never be able to make scones and wheaten bread like you did!

So , Mum, there are days when I still wish you were here and we could all just turn the clock back. But I must be thankful that you were spared seeing some things in the world of today and I am truly thankful that, although you will always hold a very special place in my heart, other friends and family members have filled many of the gaps left by your absence. God has provided and I know He always will.

With lots of love and virtual hugs

Heather xx

No, life is not all plain sailing and living on one's own can be a real struggle.

It is at such more solitary times, however, that I appreciate again the relationship that we, as Christians, have with the living Lord Jesus. One day during a busy time in my life, as I sat alone, I composed a letter to Him to express my gratitude for His constant presence in my life.

Dear Lord,

Thank you for this space. Thank you for this place. The sun is shining and so is my heart. You have given me the gift of time and quietness, of stillness before you. And in this time I allow myself to enjoy being alone. For some, aloneness is a constant burden. Many, even this morning, long for company and their only friend is the TV. For them, being alone is not a luxury but a dread. But for me, Lord, in the midst of my busy schedule, aloneness is actually a gift. Solitude, especially here in this peaceful place, with comforts all around, is ultimate enjoyment. Forgive me that I do not always think like this - I am so often ungrateful and wanting more.

Thank you for this morning. Thank you, too, Lord, for the realisation that my life and yours aren't so very different. When you were on earth, you sought times of solitude. You had many demands on your time; it sometimes seemed that everyone was around you at once. And yet, often in the midst of those busiest of busy days, you found time to be alone. Alone with your thoughts, alone with your Father, alone and yet very much in touch with the world around you.

Lord, as in all things, I want my life to be more and more like yours. I want to learn when to take time out, I want to learn how to enjoy such times, how to say no to other apparently pressing demands. I want to be like you and seek out times apart on a regular basis. But I need your help not to sink into despair on the days when I feel all alone.

So thank you, Lord, for today. For friends, for family, for interesting activities in which to be involved, for lively conversations with people I've known for years and others whom I've only just met. But above all, thank you for solitude. And the wonderful realisation that aloneness does not necessarily mean loneliness because even in our solitary times, you are there.

Your loving child,

Heather

One memorable experience of God's presence in a time of solitude came during a five-week trip to Jerusalem which I was privileged to make as my placement for a course at Bible College. Early one morning I had set out to visit the Garden Tomb on my own. Having been there a few days previously with a group, I looked forward to a time of personal reflection in this most serene of settings, which is widely believed to be the site of the Lord Jesus' resurrection.

Arriving at the gate of the garden just as dawn was breaking I was very disappointed to find it locked. There was no one about. I was about to turn sadly away when my eye caught the wording above the gate: "He is not here. He is risen." It was as if the Risen Lord Himself was speaking to me. I was reminded that I didn't need to come to any particular place, no matter how special, to find Him. Because He has risen, and ascended, and has sent His Holy Spirit into the world, we can now experience His presence anywhere. 'Hallelujah!' I thought then and 'Hallelujah' I think now as I spend time alone in much more mundane places nearer home.

A FORK IN THE ROAD

The alarm was set for an early rise. The half-hour drive to school gave me time to adjust my thinking from home to work. The bell rang at 9am and up to 30 little bodies would tumble into the classroom. Before they would tumble out again at 3pm, there would have been lots of action, interaction, chat and laughter as we shared a learning environment and discovered life truths together. Most days I loved teaching. It was a satisfying and often rewarding job, even though it was arduous much of the time.

However, 20+ years into my career, I began to feel the need of a change. Many of my married female colleagues had already had at least one break from the classroom because of maternity leave but, except for a short time of secondment, I had seldom been off for more than a day or two at once. Gradually God began to speak to me about doing something different. I wondered if I should apply for a career break. Then one evening a friend invited me to hear a special speaker in her church. Before he began to preach, the visitor outlined the benefits of the Bible School of which he was principal and invited us all to consider attending for a year's course. Like a light bulb going on in my head, I suddenly thought

'If I had a career break, I could go to Bible College'.

This was immediately followed by another inner voice telling me how stupid an idea that was – after all, wasn't I approaching 50? Wasn't I too old to study? Did I want to give up prospects of further promotion in school? But the thought persisted and I felt it was a call from God. So it was that, a few months later, I found myself enrolled as a full-time student at Bible College. It was to be a life-changing experience.

Arriving at the College just a few months before my 50th birthday, I feared I would be by far the oldest student there. But God had all that in hand too! Unknown to me, three other ladies of similar vintage had enrolled for the year on the same course. We soon became affectionately known as the 'Oldie Goldies' to some of our fellow students and we enjoyed every minute of it. As time went on, I realised that I never thought much about the respective ages of other students. Neither, surprisingly, did I particularly notice the varying colours of their skin. It was such a rich experience to share time with people from many different countries and from backgrounds a million miles apart from mine. Hearing a Polish girl pray in her own language – a first experience for me – or trying to hold a conversation in English with a guy from Bhutan who had only just arrived in UK, or discovering the strange eating preferences of the students from USA, were all aspects of a whole new world to me. God widened my horizons greatly during that year.

The word I would use most to describe my time in Bible College would be 'privilege'. I was so blessed to have many rich experiences in the company of such an international group but also, of course, to learn so much new from the Word of God as we studied together. I often reflect on those two years (for the initial one led into a second) and realise that had I been married with a family, I might not have been there at all or would certainly have been greatly curtailed in the activities to which I gave my time. Having said that, part of the richness of the experience was to meet both singles and families in College and to enjoy the children's company as well as that of their parents. I do remember one or two incidents when my age loomed large in my mind. One example was when a fellow from Colombia took out some photos of his family at home to show round the lunch table. With horror, I realised I was older than his mother! This was only to be surpassed by a chap from the Middle East telling me one day he envied me because I was nearer to the glory than he was.

All in all, Bible College was a change of direction for me. The second year afforded me the opportunity for my placement in Jerusalem and I also benefitted greatly from a Counselling Course taken that year. It was during those months that I began to question whether or not I would return to teaching or whether God had other plans to do a 'new thing' in my life at that stage. In a remarkable way, He soon showed me what that new direction was to be.

The entrance to the Bible College I attended is one-way and lies over a small narrow bridge. In those final months of my time of study, I began to see that entrance as a metaphorical picture of my arrival and impending departure from the campus. Increasingly I felt that return to school would not be my next step but I had to trust the Lord as to where else my journey might lead. One day I wrote a poem, essentially addressed to God but really just echoing my thoughts at that time.

Across the Bridge

Lord, it's almost two years now since I crossed the bridge.
That bridge that holds only one-way traffic,
That bridge that spans the gulf between the past and the future,
That bridge that brought me to Bible College.

Lord, it was the last bridge I crossed on my journey here.
It seemed pretty big all those years ago.
But then – that was good, because it was big enough for me to cross
back again if I wanted to.

Why, then, does the bridge seem increasingly narrow now?
Why does it seem so much smaller?
Could it be because You have brought me over several bridges since?
Bridges leading to those new green pastures which are always ahead
for the sheep who follow the Shepherd?

It's further now to look back to that first bridge.
And from here, everyone seems to be coming the one way.
Lord, I'm getting just a little perturbed that maybe I'll never go back over
that particular bridge again.
So, where to now? Surely not BBC for ever?!

But it's now I realise it wasn't just Bible College I crossed into two years
ago, it was a journey of faith.
And somehow I know, Lord, that the path You're leading me on has to
go on and not back.
There must be a bridge ahead I haven't seen yet.
So, Lord, wherever that bridge leads to, I want to tell You I'm ready to
cross it.

Well, almost!

God is never slow in directing His children in the way they should go. With me it happened quite unexpectedly one evening as I attended a committee meeting at our local Scripture Union HQ. Since my involvement with SU in Primary School, I had maintained a close link with the work of the SU movement and was currently serving on a committee dealing with schools' ministry. We had all but finished the meeting when the chairman announced that SU would soon be looking for a new part-time member of staff to assist especially in Primary Schools work. My ears pricked up! After the meeting I spoke to the chairperson and the wheels began to turn from there. Hence I began my ministry with SU in the following September and once again was able to thank God for the freedom I had as a single person to do a 'career swerve' later in life, even though I knew that financially it posed a slight risk as I looked to the future.

Ten happy years later, I finally retired from both Scripture Union and paid work and entered the more relaxed world of retirement. For many of my contemporaries, this stage of life consists of gardening, golf and grandchildren – or any permutations of the same. For me, I enjoy the first, dabble in the second but have, of course, no opportunity for the third. Herein lies another source of pain or disappointment for some older singles. It can be difficult when we are in the company of others whose main interest is their grandchildren. Whereas it is often fun to hear about what 3-year-old Amelia said or where Tom wants to go on his next holiday, it is not always easy to maintain a genuine conversation when you have nothing similar to contribute and only wish you had. Strangely, I have felt the experience of having no grandchildren more keenly than that of missing out on motherhood earlier in life.

Having recognised that children were not going to be the natural outcome of my way of life, there was a time when I felt disappointed and not a little apprehensive. Inevitably, questions arose such as

'Who will look after me when I get old or if I become sick?' or

'Who can I actually depend on to be there for me no matter what?' Deeper than that came questioning as to why God would have allowed this situation. I wouldn't say I've fully worked through these issues yet but I am more content now in later life to trust God to provide for me in every way as it becomes necessary.

As well as learning to rest in God, I have come to realise the wonderful fact that I have some younger friends who see me as their 'mother'. One of them recently sent me a message saying simply 'Happy Mother's Day'. She is not without a natural mum but nevertheless enjoys calling me Mummy sometimes. Similar situations exist with a few other young ladies and I love it. I believe it is God's compensation to me for not having a family of my own.

One of these friends is a single 30-something girl whom I met because of our shared experience of the Bible College. She now lives back at home in a developing country. Her lifestyle is simple but in this modern world we can nevertheless communicate by text and phone. I don't often write her a real letter but if I did, it would read something like this:

Dear Kim

I hope you are well today. I plan to be in touch with you by phone again next week but in the meantime, I have decided to write you a letter for a change.

I just wanted to say thanks for all that your friendship means to me. I have learnt such a lot since I've got to know you! Hearing about your home situation, seeing occasional pictures and just talking to you has opened up a whole new world to me about life in a country so different from UK. I find it fascinating.

*But it is also on a spiritual level that you have widened my horizons. This morning I was reading Paul's words in Philippians 4 "In whatever circumstances I am in, I have learned to be content" and I immediately thought 'That's Kim. She is content even though her circumstances are not the easiest.' I know you have actually had to **learn** to be content since you returned from the UK, because life here was more comfortable and you had more of this world's goods. But now I see you thankful for everything and trusting God for all your needs, and that is what inspires me.*

I am especially impressed by the way you handle the fact that you are not yet married, which is such an unusual situation in your culture. Even in that, you are content to let God be God and to accept cheerfully the life He has ordained for you. I for one am so glad you are single because it gives me more opportunities to enjoy your friendship and I think we understand each other because of our similar circumstances. I trust it may be so for a long time to come – although if you did decide to get married I would be very excited because I would definitely want to come to your wedding! I don't expect you will be coming to mine (joke!) but maybe some day soon you will be back for a visit and that would be just great. You know you will always be welcome here.

In the meantime, I'll look forward to speaking to you across the miles again soon.

With love and prayer,

Mummy Heather

TRAVELLING COMPANIONS

Being on one's own in life brings choices. Not least in the area of friendships. Some who are without marriage partners or children find it hard to be around those who have both. There is a temptation to cut oneself off and retreat into friendship groups of singles only. However, in my case, I have found it very stimulating to have both friends who are single and friends who are married. The importance to me of knowing some families really well is possibly not appreciated by those who take me to their hearts and homes in this way, but I know my life would be impoverished without them. Perhaps the best way I can express this is in the form of another letter. It is written to a fictitious couple but nevertheless represents all that is good in some real relationships.

Dear Pete and Sandra

On this Valentine's Day I just wanted to write you a little note of thanks. I know, Sandra, you sent me a birthday card last week and I did appreciate it, but that is not the reason for this letter. Today it is not for any tangible gift or card I want to thank you, but rather for all that both of you have given me as you've shared your lives with me over the years. I'm sure none of us wants to count up how many years it is since we first knew each other, but then that is all part of what makes me grateful for your friendship. It has been such a faithful friendship, through many differing circumstances in all our lives.

To be honest, I cannot say that about all my married friends. Some of them – male and female, but mostly the latter, naturally – were so much closer to me when we were all single, but somehow have let the friendship drift since their marriage separated us into two different lifestyles. I suppose it always takes so much more effort to reach out to those who are a bit different from ourselves.

So thank you, Sandra, for maintaining our bond of friendship down through the years, and thank you, Pete, for accepting me so readily not just as your wife's friend, but as a Christian sister to whom you also show genuine affection and whose company you say you value. I have so enjoyed the many chats we have had and the laughs we have shared.

As I reflect on all of this, though, I realise that the richness of our relationships with each other is in no small measure due to the fact that you and I both know that you are very secure in your marriage bond. You are so at ease with each other that it becomes a delight to spend time with you and see God's love modelled in a way that we singles do not experience every day.

I have loved being with you when the family are around, and being made to feel part of it, with all the banter and teasing that that involves. Thank you for sharing so much, especially the more serious side of family life, as we have talked together about some of the heartaches involved as the children have grown up. How lovely now to be looking forward to the day out at Susie's wedding in the summer. She will be such a beautiful bride. I guess all I would wish for Susie and Ben as they start out on married life is that they would have as happy a marriage as you, Pete and Sandra, and that, like you, they would see marriage not only as an exclusive and private relationship – although it must be that at times of course – but also as an added opportunity to extend God's love to those on the outside of marriage who might appreciate it as I do.

May the Lord bless you so much for all the blessing you are to me.

With love in Him

Heather

Relationships form such a vital part of life that we will almost certainly find some of our greatest joys through them but we also experience some of our deepest anguish because of them. Throughout my adult life, I have met and mingled with many other people. I would say I have a considerable range of acquaintances. However, an acquaintance is a far cry from a friend and a casual friend is not the same as a close friend. It is when we allow ourselves to be vulnerable and we open up to others about who we really are and what we really feel, that we can experience true joy on the one hand but risk considerable hurt on the other.

Perhaps uniquely in singleness circles, some of us find difficulty in maintaining true friendships with everyone. Lacking a marriage partner, there is a danger that we look to each other for affirmation and affection. When relationships intertwine in a singles group, this can lead to difficulties and it is a challenge to avoid jealousies on the one hand and exclusiveness on the other. Only the Lord Jesus can protect us from these follies and enable us to live in freedom. For others, same-sex attraction – whether real or imagined – can play a part in spoiling healthy relationships.

In thinking of these issues, and in order to try to verbalise what I appreciate about my closest friendships, I took to the letter-writing pad again. I think all single people should have a friend like Paula. They are blessed if they do.

Dear Paula

It's not often you get a letter from me! Neither do we often compliment each other, as you know. Ours is the sort of friendship where we almost take one another for granted and we know each other so well that we seldom think to say words of appreciation.

However, surprise, surprise! I want to write you this note today because, as you know, I'm trying to record a bit of my life story, telling people my thoughts about singleness. As I was writing the other day, I got to thinking about how all single people need close friendships and how much lonelier life would be without them. We do tend to depend on relationships with other singles for emotional support, don't we? And, of course, it's good to have like-minded company to socialise with or to chat things over.

You, my dear friend Paula, tick all these boxes and more. We've laughed together, cried together, studied together, just been together for a good number of years now. Hopefully you've got some benefit at least from my company over the years but this is just to tell you – in case you were ever in any doubt – that I've benefitted greatly from yours. As you are all too aware, I'm no saint but all I can say is that if I hadn't had your friendship I guess I'd be a lot worse in many ways!

So here's to many more laughs, tears, chats and outings, for as long as we're both able.

Love and prayers,

Heather

All friends are a blessing, whether long term or short term, whether those with whom we spend a lot of time or those we know only because we share a particular hobby or interest. In the Christian life, church friends are often special. I am always thankful that in our church there are several of us who are of a certain age and enjoy one another's company. It is not unusual for a group of us to go out for an evening together or look out for each other at church events. As well as that, I'm privileged to know one or two couples well enough to spend time in their homes occasionally or be comfortable to go with them on an outing. None of us thinks there always has to be a fourth person to even things up!

As a single person, especially as I've grown older, I have come to appreciate my church family more and more. Collectively, church friends are a unique bunch. We talk of the 'church family' and that can be a true description, in that churches bring together people of all ages and differing backgrounds in a way that few other groupings do. I count among my church friends some who are in a totally different age bracket from myself. One of them is about six! As in any family, some members relate better to one another than do others, and at times there is real tension between certain parties. However, just as in our human families, we are all bound together and have to at least make an effort to get on with one other. I sometimes marvel at how Jesus maintained unity amongst His 12 closest friends when they were all so different from each other! He is still in the business of enabling people to unite under His Lordship.

Although I may never love my church friends all dearly, and there are some who are more like distant cousins than close siblings, nevertheless it is a joy to belong to such a fellowship and to know acceptance within it. Now I feel compelled to write them a letter too…

Dear Church Family

Sorry for this rather impersonal way of addressing you but it would be impossible to name you all individually. It would also be impossible for me to thank each one of you for the huge contribution you have made to my life. Collectively you have influenced me in ways you may never have realised.

As you probably know, I am single and I live on my own. I don't have a lot of 'family time' most weeks although I am always made very welcome in the homes of my siblings and a few close friends when I visit their families. So church life is very important to me. There I meet my spiritual family. You truly are my brothers and sisters in Christ.

As in any human family we don't always all agree about everything and, of course, there are some of you I am closer to than others, but basically I love you all in the Lord. It means a lot to me to have all the generations interacting together, whether in worship or Bible Study or in fun activities. Those of us on our own do appreciate being part of such a fellowship.

So thank you. Thanks especially to those who make a special effort from time to time to sacrifice some of your own family time so that you can be part of a church family activity. Your presence can make all the difference. Please keep on being the wonderful church members that you are. I'm proud to be one of you!

Blessings

Heather

Church, of course, is not just a social club, important though that aspect is. Primarily it is a place of teaching and learning, of preaching and worship. We are blessed in our fellowship with leaders who expound the

Word of God to us faithfully on a regular basis. Many topics are covered in the Scriptures and through the course of a year, we will have been caused to think Biblically about lots of them. However, on the subject of love and marriage, I have not often heard a sermon which 'scratches where I itch'. That's why I was delighted one Sunday, when visiting a friend's church, to discover that the pastor was speaking from 1 Corinthians 7 and particularly about marriage and singleness. As I listened, I was struck by the fact – and grateful for it – that God has included sexual matters in His Word and has given us clear guidance to follow.

Life in the secular world has become more complicated in recent years and much of it has infiltrated the Christian world. The current debate over the redefinition of marriage has caused concern and confusion in many church circles. For single Christians, it has raised issues formerly unknown or unspoken of in the church.

For example, in the secular world, homosexuality has become ever more acceptable, and 'single' often merely means 'available' or 'free of ties'. Neither necessarily means a life of celibacy. For those of us who are Christians, however, if we are without a marriage partner, the future is one of celibacy and we pray for the grace to accept that. I have found it interesting, on several occasions, when holidaying with a female friend, that we have been offered a double-bedded room, on the assumption that that is what we prefer.

When I heard the preacher in my friend's church expound the clear teaching of 1 Corinthians, I was grateful that God has given us such boundaries to help us live in the best way. Had St Paul been a contemporary writer, I may have been tempted to email him about what I had heard that Sunday morning, but of course I knew that was impossible. So I wrote this letter instead.

Dear Paul,

Thank you for your letter. You wrote it so long ago that you'd maybe be surprised to have a reply at this time. Mind you, even for me it's a record. I'm not known for answering letters too quickly but I've never waited for nearly 2000 years before writing back to anyone! However, having just re-read your letter – or part of it – which was written not directly to me at all but to the friends you knew at Corinth, I feel compelled to say thank you to you.

Firstly, thank you for taking the time and trouble to write to those guys. If it weren't for the letters you sent them, we'd be a lot poorer spiritually these days. I wonder did you ever think that what you wrote would have such a long-lasting and vital impact on thousands of people's lives. I for one am so grateful that you wrote at all, and especially for some of the topics you chose to write about.

The one I have in mind today, since I read your letter again yesterday, is singleness. Actually you never called it that. You spoke about people being married or unmarried, or being virgins. I guess in your day, singleness as a lifestyle was less established and it really was unusual for folk not to get married.

When I think of that, I'm even more thankful that you dared to tackle the subject in your letter to the Corinthian church. It's not a subject many talk openly about in churches even today, and because of that, many of us who are unmarried find it a bit difficult to tell others how we feel about it. On reading your letter yesterday, I was really struck by the fact that you were so honest about the different issues surrounding marriage – or the lack of it.

It's good to recognise, as you did, that God has not given any definite command to those who remain single. It is not that we must, or must not, eventually enter into a marriage relationship. That's a freeing thought. Isn't God so good in the freedom He allows us in so many aspects of our lives? I know that as a Jew you appreciated that more than most. Laws can so easily become a bind, but Jesus showed us the God of grace, who grants us freedom and reminds us we are all unique individuals.

Thank you that in your letter you also took that tone. You talked about each state as valid and pleasing to God, rather than exalting one over the other. In fact, your whole discourse on the single life was so balanced, that I found it refreshingly helpful. As you said, there certainly can be advantages in living as an unmarried person. None of us finds it easy to keep God's priorities in mind all through our lives and to live according to His designs, but it is certainly true that when one is not married there is more possibility of concentrating on such ideals and of finding time to do so. Even Mary and Martha in Jesus' day showed that could be done – they never seemed to stop thinking of how they could make Him more comfortable or help Him somehow in His ministry. I wonder if people would ever say that about me as an unmarried person.

But then, Paul, you also recognised there were challenges for those who did not marry. Thank you for addressing the question of celibacy. It's not one which is mentioned too often either, but it's a major consideration for single people. In fact, now that I have re-read your letter myself, I think I must encourage a few of my younger friends to read it too. (I know you'd love for that to happen!) There's so much good advice in there for those who are struggling with the idea of long-term singleness.

It's a reminder to us all that, as always with God, there's no middle road in these things. The teaching of the world these days says there are lots of options, and I'm sure the folk in Corinth had tried out a good few of them in your day, but I'm glad to be reminded that God's word on the subject is unchanging. It's the whole package with Him. Singleness and celibacy or marriage and intimacy. That's why, as you say, we all need to decide which it's to be. I do love your straight talking – there's no room for wondering what you meant when we've read your letters, Paul!

Anyhow, I must end this one of mine. I know you would write letters much longer than this, but then you covered lots of topics at once. I just wanted to thank you for the way you dealt with this one particular subject.

I look forward to meeting you some day – not too soon I hope,

Yours in Christ

Heather Henry

Sadly, not all public speakers or writers in the Christian world are so well attuned to the needs of single people. I quite often attend conferences and conventions, where the Bible is expounded or Biblical topics are explored. On one such occasion, some years ago, I was both horrified and disappointed by a speaker who had apparently been asked to address the topic of 'Godly Family Living'. He chose to read from Ephesians 5. Although his audience was drawn from many different backgrounds and represented a myriad of lifestyles, this dear man spoke to us as if we all lived in the 'perfect' family of Mum, Dad, and 2.5 children. I almost expected to hear mention of the dog, the cat and the rabbit. Only once did he remark that 'some, of course, never marry' and I never heard him concede that some couples do not have children. Needless to say, it was not the best convention evening I've ever experienced! I felt compelled to write a letter afterwards to the organiser of the programme.

Dear Administrator

I enclose a small donation towards the work of Fresh New Day. *I really enjoyed the event this year and benefitted greatly from both the teaching and the fellowship. There is, however, one comment I would like to make regarding the content of the Evening Gathering on the theme of 'Godly Family Living'.*

Although I appreciate that Ephesians 5 deals primarily with marriage and children and it was understandable that the bulk of the speaker's talk would therefore be addressed to couples, nevertheless I would have to say that I was disappointed that many important issues were either entirely ignored or glossed over very quickly. Singleness and childlessness were the two most obvious of these. It is my impression that it is difficult for many happily married folk in the church today to identify with either of these topics, perhaps including the speaker that evening.

Because many such issues are not generally addressed in local churches, I feel that Fresh New Day *could be an excellent place to explore them. May I propose then, that in a future year we might have a seminar devoted to the variety of lifestyles Christians may face. This could include some of the following topics:*

- *Marriage*
- *Divorce*
- *Marriage to a non-Christian partner*
- *Living together in a non-married relationship*
- *Singleness.*

As a single person, naturally my particular desire is to see that topic covered. I believe that many of us see our single lifestyle not as a 'problem' but rather as a legitimate alternative to marriage. The older I become, the more I feel it is important that we share positive insights about singleness with younger people, and encourage them to realise that it just may be God's will for them to remain unmarried. It may also be helpful for some married folk to hear a little more about this subject, especially those whose ministry includes single people. Likewise, I'm sure it would be good to address the issue of childlessness in a positive way, acknowledging that it is a situation encountered by many Christian couples.

Thank you for all you do in preparation for each Fresh New Day *event. I'll be very grateful if the organising committee will give consideration to the idea of including some of the topics I've mentioned, over the next couple of years.*

Yours sincerely

Heather Henry

Naturally, because I am unmarried, that is the lens through which I view the world and so I sometimes hear things differently from others who are married. However, the Word of God is not restricted and it speaks to us all in our own circumstances. Whatever our relationships, Jesus calls us all to Himself with a gracious invitation. He invites us to come and be satisfied first and foremost in Him. I thank God for those over the years who have told me of this invitation and have opened up God's Word to me so that I have seen its truth and been encouraged to respond to Jesus' call on my life. I trust that this will be so until He finally calls me Home to Himself. Perhaps I can best sum up my gratitude for the past and my hope for the future in the words of Horatio Bonar's ancient hymn "I heard the voice of Jesus say". Its final verse reads like this:

I heard the voice of Jesus say
'I am this dark world's Light:
Look unto me, thy morn shall rise
And all thy day be bright.'
I looked to Jesus and I found
In Him my Star, my Sun
And in that Light of life I'll walk
Till travelling days are done.

JOURNEY'S END... NOT!

Almost everyone likes a happy ending to a story. We love the idea that we will all 'live happily ever after' no matter what the obstacles have been along the way. Those who live the single life often long that their particular life story will eventually end with Prince/Princess Charming sweeping them off their feet and the two of them disappearing into the sunset together. But real life is seldom so tidy in its ending. Yes, I have known of some friends who have married somewhat unexpectedly 'later in life' and have experienced much joy in a marriage relationship after many years of singleness. But for many others, earthly life holds no such happy ending and, indeed, difficulties can increase as age takes its toll.

The death of each of my parents was a traumatic event in my life. Many years later, I still remember them both with much affection and it disturbs me when I sometimes dream about them and waken to such disappointment that they are not actually there. As a single person, however, I will never know or fully understand the deep pain of losing a life partner. Widowhood is one situation I will not experience. Moreover, as a female, I can understand even less what it is like for a man to lose his wife through death. I have, nevertheless, wept alongside both men and women as they have grieved the loss of beloved spouses and none of us has been ashamed of our tears.

The wonder of the gospel is such that, despite desperate sadness, when we must part from those whom we have loved the most, we can have hope that this is not the end. 'Tears may endure for a night but joy will come in the morning.' As I meet with friends who are widowed, both men and women, and try to walk alongside them as they face huge readjustments in experiencing a new form of singleness on the death of their life partner, it is wonderful to be able to share hope with them, even if I cannot fully empathise with their loss. As Christians, we all know that death is not the end and that one day we will be joyfully reunited with all those who love the Lord and have put their trust in Him. Many questions still surround the mystery of heaven but we are assured that it will be a place of ultimate joy and fulfilment, where sin is banished and all is good.

In thinking of these things one evening, I found it therapeutic to compose a letter to very good friend who has 'gone on before' some years ago, but whose company I still miss and whose memory I cherish. It seems fitting as I draw to a close in this reflection of my life, to finish up with that letter. Perhaps it sums up, better than any other writing could do, the hope that I have in Christ as I continue on this single-track path on which He has led me so far.

It has not all been easy – because that is the common lot of us all, Christian or otherwise. But as I look back to age 37 and way beyond it, I can only be thankful for God's goodness and faithfulness to me, not least in being my constant companion, friend, protector and guide throughout the years.

I doubt very much that I shall have another 37 years (or that if I did I would remember much of them!) but I do know that for however many it may be, Jesus Christ will be with me and He will not change.

For I have His promise in the Bible, in what I have always considered to be my 'life verse':

Hebrews 13 v 8

"Jesus Christ is the same yesterday, today and forever."

To Him be the glory.

Dear Jeanette

Last night I had a wonderful dream – or maybe it was a vision. You were the centre of it. How I wished this morning that I could have phoned you to tell you all about it. I really miss chatting things over with you. We used to do that so often, as you will remember. Well, I'm not sure what you remember now actually, as heaven is still a little bit of a mystery to me. But I do know you are now blissfully happy. My dream last night confirmed that, and it was so good to be able to imagine you fitting into what the Bible tells us is in store up ahead for those who know and love the Lord.

The picture of you in my dream was not of an angelic being with a harp, but of you, my friend Jeanette, still recognisable, working away happily as you worshipped the Lord of glory. Remember – well, I do – when we learnt that the Hebrew words for 'work' and 'worship' were the same, 'Avodah'. It's all tied up together both here and there. But last night I saw, too, that you were well rested in spite of the work there was to do. After all, there's no effort now in work, is there? It's just continuous worship. It was certainly a joy for me to see you so content.

Another thing I remember about our chats long ago was the sense of discontent we both felt at times – in our work, in our families, and maybe mostly because we were 'on the shelf'. How many times we used to moan about having no man around the house, and always being in female company. We must have wasted a lot of time on talking about 'that' subject.

And now, just a short few years later, I am discovering that life can be lived without a male partner and you have long since ceased to be concerned about any such matters. You are in that place where relationships are all perfect and what happened on earth as regards marriages is no longer relevant. I could see in my dream that you were truly satisfied and fulfilled, but so were all the others around you. There was no way of telling who had been married or who hadn't in a previous life. It just didn't feature.

So, Jeanette, I guess what I've learnt from my glimpse into your present wonderful world, is not to get too hung up on any subject in the days which remain to me, but to think of their importance – or otherwise – in the light of eternity. From now on, I'm going to try to see everything from this point of view. If God chooses to bring a husband into my life even at this stage, so be it. But, hey, I don't need a man in order to practise working and worshipping. Avodah is a personal activity, regardless of one's marital state.

Right now, I'm off to practise some resting. Perhaps I'll dream about you again tonight, who knows? Anyhow, I'll really look forward to seeing you again one day. If it weren't for being misunderstood by some down here, I'd add to that 'the sooner the better'.

In the meantime, another Hebrew word. 'Mizpah' – The Lord watch between you and me while we are absent from one another.

In His love,

Heather

APPENDIX

Life in Lockdown

The bulk of this book was written before the outbreak of the Covid-19 coronavirus. It is now April 2020 and the world has changed. Almost every country is, or has been, in some form of lockdown – a word we hardly knew until a month or two ago. We have been asked to self-isolate (another new word in our global vocabulary) as far as possible. This, we have discovered, just means Stay At Home!

So how is it for those of us by ourselves when all one can do is to stay inside one's own property unless venturing out for essential supplies or a bout of daily exercise?

Suffice to say, lockdown is a challenge for everyone. A single mum with three children living in a third floor apartment has a huge job to do; the elderly couple who are both a little frail, and normally dependent on seeing family members on a regular basis, have difficult adjustments to make; and the church pastor who can no longer be engaged in either face to face personal work or preaching to a gathered congregation can feel very frustrated. No one gets it easy during such a period.

For me, it has been interesting to realise just how much I usually depend on being in company. Whereas I am reasonably used to my own company, because I live alone, nevertheless it is different when I know that I can't just hop in the car and go to visit someone or meet up with a friend for coffee. It has thrown me back not only on my own inner resources but primarily on my relationship with God. Friends are still available from time to time on the phone or through various forms of social media but the only constant companion is the Lord Jesus.

I finished the original book by saying that I knew that, whatever time I had left on earth, He would be with me. Little did I think when I wrote that, that I would now have such an unexpected opportunity to prove it to be true. But that is where I am at as I write – taking each day as it comes, remembering those who have a much harder life than I at the moment and being thankful that I have a home to Stay At.

And so we go on trusting the One who, for reasons known only to Him, has allowed this worldwide pandemic with its horrific consequences for so many. May He help each of us to live out all our remaining days to His glory, whatever our circumstances, even when these circumstances lead us on a road, not just less travelled, but never travelled before.

Proverbs 4:18

The path of the righteous is like the morning sun,

shining ever brighter till the full light of day.